Left blank intentionally

PROSPERITY
delusion

by
Dr. Marc Garcia

MBG Publishing

Published by MBG Publishing

Copyright 2020 by Marc Garcia

MBG Publishing
P.O. Box 1318
Lyman, SC 29365

All Rights Reserved

No part of this book may be reproduced or transmitted in any form or by any means, electronic or mechanical, including photocopying, recording or by any information storage or retrieval system without written permission from Marc Garcia, except for the inclusion of brief quotations in a review.

For more information on ordering copies of Prosperity Delusion and other ministry items contact The Bridge Ministries at (864) 469-0837 or visit www.bethebridgesc.org.

All scripture references versions are noted with scripture and may include from the King James Version, New King James Version, Message Bible, New International Version, and Literal Translation Bible.

ISBN: 978-0-9884703-4-7

CONTENTS

Introduction	1
Redeeming Every Area	5
The Genesis of Luxury	25
The Quest for Provision	35
There Is A Place	45
Perception - What Do You See?	53

Acknowledgments:

First and foremost thank you to my Lord and Savior – Jesus for all He has done in my life. Grace, mercy, and joy has truly been my portion.

I would like to thank those who help build my faith foundation; Nestor, Freddy, Kenneth, Jesse, and others. Whose voices still echo in my faith words as I share. Who set the foundation for this book by showing what prosperity it about and pushing me more than 20 years ago to go deeper.

Lastly want to thank my lovely wife who worked arduously with me on this project. The patience, and fortitude to get it done has been amazing. Thank you for loving the Christ in me.

A WORD FROM THE AUTHOR

There is a people looking for more depth to the Word of God. Many feel in their heart that there must be more.

Many live their lives searching for more. More of this, more of that, yet the challenge is that many are searching for something that is already made available to them. What is required, is what the Apostle Paul suggests to each of us, the renewing of our mind.

This topic of prosperity has become a taboo subject. Many reject it because there have been some who have taken it to an unbalanced level. Others have taken it to the extreme focusing solely on money, however in this book we are going to see something different, we are going to take a journey together into the renewal of our mind concerning this word – Prosperity.

First, prosperity is the design of the God who supplies. Prosperity is not only money, nor is it only spiritual, but moreover a both/and.

My desire in sharing this revelation is to dispel the delusion concerning this message about prosperity that we have heard for so long.

The scripture tells us in God's voice, "My people are destroyed for lack of knowledge." This is vital information for the individual's growth. People perish because the vital information needed for growth has been distorted resulting in much confusion in the Body of Christ.

I am an avid believer that authors like myself, must point to scripture for answers. I further this belief with the statement that this book is not an attempt to answer all questions but my hope is to entice you to build upon the revelation for your own personal growth. I believe every Christian author should do this.

One more item before we enter this journey. I love to share revelation. I am a staunch believer that there is no greater gift I can give than wisdom. Often this wisdom is in form of a book. I share this because I want you to know that this book was originally written in Spanish, and then I translated it to English (one of the blessings of being bilingual). Due to paradigms, cultures and level of immersion in the prosperity message being so different between these two demographics, it would have been an injustice to translate it literally without considering the differences of the readers. My hope is that you understand the essence of the message is the same, yet some license was used to expand more in one language than the other.

Personally, I have paid a price in chasing prosperity in the financial sense, all the while neglecting the riches of a healthy family. I worked hard and long only to overlook them at times in the process. Yet as always in hindsight, I learned the lesson in my process. With God, I came out of the process victorious over the prosperity delusion.

You are blessed,

Dr. Marc Garcia

1
Trading Paradigms

Revealed knowledge is what the Apostle Paul calls, precise wisdom/knowledge. There are many things that we believe simply because someone in authority over our life has shown or shared a concept with us. Since we held a person in high respect, we never asked questions. Yet, there is a grand difference between asking a question, and questioning with doubt or debate due to unbelief.

When a revelation is presented that does not match our paradigm, we must analyze it. As a believer, we must discern and decide if it is the Word of God being revealed or man-made revelation. Based on the result, if it is the Word of God, we as believers, do not have the luxury of not making it our own solely because it does not match our paradigm.

The Word of God must be our final and concluding authority. It must be above every opinion, conjecture, or assumption. When this is in place, the result is a revealed TRUTH replacing an assumed truth.

The delusion many have embraced in the Body of Christ is that prosperity is all about money. God does not want you poor or going through lack. The tendency is to believe this delusion as fact because it has come from a genuine ministry leader who (I believe) has your best interests in mind. However, we as listeners tend to take things to the extreme. The erroneous belief that prosperity is solely based on the abundance of our financial resources is a delusion which we will dispel together.

Let's see what the Word of God has to say about prosperity to either prove or disprove this delusion.

Let me begin with a question. How many of you want to fulfill, live and walk out the will of God? I would imagine we all do. I do not believe there is any person reading this whom does not desire to fulfill the will of the Father. So, here is a follow up question. If you discover that it is the will of God to prosper you, would you do His will? Here is where many are challenged, simply because they have a preconceived idea about what prosperity is. Based on incomplete information they have a paradigm that refutes the truth about prosperity.

For this reason, let us first look at the true definition of prosperity. As per Webster's Dictionary, the definition of prosperity is the condition of being successful or thriving.

It is the design of God to supply for us. Many in the church comprehend this truth. God is our supplier. Later we will talk about the well-known Jehovah Jireh reference. So now the question would then be, what does God supply for us?

> **PROSPERITY IS THE CONDITION OF BEING SUCCESSFUL OR THRIVING**

To be able to answer this question, we must return to the prime gift He supplied for us - a Savior - Jesus. Then we need to understand what was encompassed in the person of this Savior named Jesus.

One key item is salvation.

The word salvation in the Greek is "soteria" and it means:
- Preservation
- Security
- Freedom

This is the sum of all the benefits and blessings that Christians have as the redeemed of the Lord. In other words, salvation is inclusive. It is not limited to a particular area in our lives. It is not that we are saved in one area and not another. We are preserved, secure, free, and we have (present tense) all the benefits that pertain to us in Christ; and it is at the ready. Just like a child has the capability to speak, but must learn his or her words and how to compile them together, this very thought pattern can be applied to these 5 areas.

We are redeemed! Which means that we have been bought with a price. Now the value of what you pay, or the cost must be equal or greater to the value of what is purchased. This is the only way HIS sacrifice would be enough for us. John 10 verse 6-11 says:

> *Jesus used this illustration, but they did not understand the things which He spoke to them. Then Jesus said to them again, "Most assuredly, I say to you, I am the door of the sheep. All who ever came before Me are thieves and robbers, but the sheep did not hear them. I am the door. If anyone enters by Me, he will be saved, and will go in and out and find pasture. The thief does not come except to steal, and to kill, and to destroy. I have come that they may have life, and that they may have it more abundantly. I am the good shepherd. The good shepherd gives His life for the sheep." (NKJV)*

The word abundantly is defined as exceeding some number or measure or rank or need; over and above, more than is necessary, super-added; superior, extraordinary, surpassing, uncommon.

In his first letter to the church in Thessalonica, Paul closes his letter in verse 23 of chapter 5 saying the following words:

And the very God of peace sanctify you wholly; and I pray God your whole spirit and soul and body be preserved blameless unto the coming of our Lord Jesus Christ. (KJV)

The translation for "sanctify you wholly" is the same word used for perfection. It is not perfection as we may think, but moreover the process of maturing. A thriving condition – in other words PROSPERING. Perhaps a better translation (in my view) of the scripture would be as follows:

And the very God of peace prosper you; and I pray God your whole spirit and soul and body be prosperous unto the coming of our Lord Jesus Christ.

As we progress, I am going to randomly remind you of the definition of prosperity, because we cannot allow the old paradigm to continue, we must change it.

Now the key point of redemption is that the price was paid in full in five specific areas of our life: our spirit, soul, body, social life and finances. Now through the price being paid we are placed in a position to prosper in these five areas. The goal of our salvation is so that we can prosper. Now I know you think that statement might be blasphemy, however, let's review. Salvation has placed us in the position to be successful or thrive. Jesus came so that we can prosper in five specific areas. Each area of our life are of equal importance, none is greater than the other, otherwise the price for the redemption would not calculate.

II
Redeeming Every Area

Since we took the time to define what redemption, salvation and prosperity truly are now we can go in deeper and discover the five areas in which God desires for us to prosper (to be successful and thriving). These five areas I believe are all inclusive since we are referring to the person, individual, and his or her walk with God.

OUR SPIRIT

Number one is our spirit (note the lowercase). God desires that our spirit prospers, that it be successful and thriving.

The psalmist says in 31:5:

> *Into thine hand I commit my spirit: thou hast redeemed me, O Lord God of truth. (KJV)*

A person's spirit before knowing the Lord is in enmity with God. God redeems us through the sacrifice of Jesus – we are redeemed or put into proper relationship anew, as we were before coming to the earth.

The redeemed spirit is the only one out of the five that is totally redeemed at the time of conversion. Note what Titus says in 3:4-7:

> *But— When God our Savior revealed his kindness and love, he saved us, not because of the righteous things we had done, but because of his mercy. He washed away our sins, giving us a new birth and new life through the Holy Spirit. He generously poured out the Spirit upon us through Jesus Christ our Savior. Because of his grace he declared us righteous and gave us confidence that we will inherit eternal life. (NLT)*

In His grace he declared us righteous. The word "declared" is in the past tense. This means that your spirit is declared righteous the moment you accept Him as Savior. What is always interesting to me is that so many hold on to the scripture, "there is none righteous." Then on the opposite spectrum there are those who are against the "prosperity message" because they say biblical prosperity is solely in the spirit. What more prosperity does your spirit need after being pulled out from the grips of hell? This is the full prosperity of the spirit. Your spirit, the moment you accept Jesus, has reached its highest level of prosperity. There is no greater level of success and thriving for your spirit, greater than allowing your spirit to be the habitation of Jesus.

OUR SOUL

What happens is that there is a great confusion between the spirit prospering and the SOUL prospering, which is the 2nd area of our life He desires for us to prosper in.

Naturally because of this confusion we must now define what the soul is. The soul is the seat of the mind, will and intellect/emotions. It is where decisions are made, where human emotions reside, as well as the logic of man. The soul's prosperity is progressive. It begins at the moment of salvation and continues as we willfully continue to "renew our mind". In fact, right now as you read this, or you receive the Word, your soul is prospering. Your soul is slowly attaining the condition of being successful or thriving. As your mind is reading and analyzing, it is processing, growing and thriving. The Apostle Paul spoke about the renewing of the mind multiple times. In Romans 12:2 he says to the Romans (who were learning something entirely new):

> *Do not be conformed to this world, but be transformed by the renewal of your mind, that by testing you may discern what is the will of God, what is good and acceptable and perfect. (ESV)*

It is interesting that the Apostle Paul notes that there is a connection between renewing of the mind and testing to discern the will of God. Essentially telling us under the direction of Holy Spirit, that when our spirit hears something from God, we discern it via our soul, and this process is the renewing of our mind.

Paul again in a very vulnerable, transparent moment, says previously these words in chapter 7 verses 14-23 concerning the soul and spirit:

> *For we know that the law is spiritual, but I am carnal, sold under sin. For what I am doing, I do not understand. For what I will to do, that I do not practice; but what I hate, that I do. If, then, I do what I will not to do, I agree with the law that it is good. But now, it is no longer I who do it, but sin that dwells in me. For I know that in me (that is, in my flesh) nothing good dwells; for to will is present with me, but how to perform what is good I do not find. For the good that I will to do, I do not do; but the evil I will not to do, that I practice. Now if I do what I will not to do, it is no longer I who do it, but sin that dwells in me. I find then a law, that evil is present with me, the one who wills to do good. For I delight in the law of God according to the inward man. But I see another law in my members, warring against the law of*

my mind, and bringing me into captivity to the law of sin which is in my members. (NKJV)

His (and our) sinful nature is not of the spirit, but our soul. He speaks about the intimate parts of who he is, he speaks of his soul; mind, will and intellect and how the same wants to do something yet his spirit says no. Why? The fully prospered or renewed spirit is in enmity with the unrenewed soul. It is for this very reason that many believers still sin and commit errors. They are not sinners, they are believers in the process of renewing themselves, otherwise known as prospering their souls (in the process of being successful or thriving in their thinking and emotions).

Let me expand this with an example. The moment you decide to accept the Lord Jesus into your heart, the scripture tells us that at that very moment we are a new creature, old things have passed. We embrace a promise of God doing something new. A wonderful promise! However, what happens in the spiritual realm? The moment you return to your seat, a new creature and all, aside from a miracle from God Himself, the memories of your past will still be there. The insecurities of your past will still be there. If you had a bad hair day, your hair will still be bad or depending on what church you go to, it may be worse after the laying on of hands. If you had problems with your kids, you will probably still have them. If you have a predisposition to smoking, it may very well be you will still have it. (Please note, yes there are cases that I have seen and heard of where people were instantly delivered.) Many times the problems may appear even greater. This is the result of a new spirit with an unrenewed soul. The is the beginning process of renewal.

OUR BODY

The third place where God has designed for us to prosper is in our bodies. Prosperity again, the condition of being successful or thriving. This time in our bodies, is extremely important for a long life. We can see this in two facets; the first one being that we prosper in the Body of Christ (the local church to which you are assigned). The second, being that we prosper in our human body. He has given us the wisdom in the Word on how to live and eat.

Romans 12:1 says the following:

> *I appeal to you therefore, brothers, by the mercies of God, to present your bodies as a living sacrifice, holy and acceptable to God, which is your spiritual worship. (ESV)*

I so enjoy this verse because there is a sense of urgency to it. Paul says to them, "brothers, by the mercy of God". In other words, there was a deep desire from him that his brothers present themselves as a living sacrifice, holy and acceptable to God. Then he continues to share how this is the way we worship. Now here is the rub, we are to present our bodies as a living sacrifice, however a body that has not been taken care of is a body that is not acceptable. The comparison he is making, is that just like the Lamb of God presented Himself as an acceptable sacrifice, we must as well. The sacrifice to be acceptable had to be without blemish, not sick, nor abused.

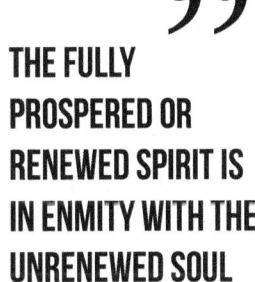

THE FULLY PROSPERED OR RENEWED SPIRIT IS IN ENMITY WITH THE UNRENEWED SOUL

2 Corinthians 6:16-17 says:

> *And what agreement has the temple of God with idols? For you are the temple of the living God. As God has said:*
>
> *"I will dwell in them and walk among them.*
>
> *I will be their God, And they shall be My people."*
>
> *Therefore, "Come out from among them and be separate, says the Lord. Do not touch what is unclean, and I will receive you." (NKJV)*

You are the temple or tabernacle of God; the dwelling place of the most high God.

In 3 John 1:2, the infamous prosperity scripture says the following:

> *Beloved, I pray that in every way you may succeed and prosper and be in good health [physically], just as [I know] your soul prospers [spiritually]. (AMP)*

When the Apostle Paul says "just as" it tells us there is a comparison. If we were to see this in context it would show us that the desire mentioned here is that our body prospers in relation with our souls. This shows us that there is a correlation of the progressive growth (prosperity) of our soul with our body. Many embrace revelation as it pertains to how to live our lives in the areas of faith, our homes and our children. Yet very seldom do we accept it as easily concerning our health.

Now, how do we prosper in our body? The same way we do in our soul, through revelation. When God speaks to you about your health and you know you have high blood-pressure then you know He desires for you to make adjustments. If you have diabetes, and He sets you up to be a part of something dealing with diabetes, then take the hint and get the information. He desires and has designed us to prosper in our bodies. Contrary to popular belief it is very rare that He wants you in heaven before the assigned time. He has designed you to fulfill something here on earth, and the way we take care of our body can thwart that fulfillment.

For many in the Body of Christ, how we view the way we eat must change. I am not speaking about a diet or fad. Diets and fads do nothing for the long term, they provide a brief result for a short term. What I am referring to are our thought patterns on food. The paradigms formed in us as children perhaps are the ones that we now carry as adults.

If you are like me, you may have been raised to finish all that is on your plate. If not, an interrogation would have been accompanied by accusations of how I may not have liked the food. My wife and I have been exposed to Foster Care training. One of the patterns we were told to look out for was food hoarding. Why? A child that has suffered extreme poverty or lack may store food for later when he or she is hungry and/or depressed. This is orphan thinking. It is based on the thought that the food supply will end, and that it would cease to exist. I share this because these are both extremes. One pattern of thought was to eat everything on your plate, because there were starving people in other countries and the other pattern is the need to store food up in case someone comes to grab it. It all stems from our fight or flight response as a human. However, when brought into equilibrium, we can see that it is OK to leave something on our plate when we are full or satisfied. As well, it is a balanced thought when I can comprehend that I do not need to hoard food. There is indeed enough and the threat of someone else coming to take it is not real.

When I allowed my mind to change concerning food, God showed me how my body could prosper. I had to learn that it is OK to leave a little food behind. I had to relearn that food is not a solution to stress. I had to relearn that perhaps I don't need that much food. I had to understand that eating is not a remedy for boredom.

As you may have noticed there is an undertone about the prosperity of the body. It is the fact that we must change our mind, to put it in biblical terms "renew our mind" concerning food.

OUR SOCIAL LIFE

The next area God has designed for us to prosper in is our social life. Our social life is the life that we live with others. His desire is that we prosper in this area so that we can love one another well.

When we operate on this level of love we are prospering.

Jesus speaks and gives us wisdom concerning this very thing in the recount of Matthew. He shares:

> *"You have heard that it was said, 'You shall love your neighbor and hate your enemy.' But I say to you, Love your enemies and pray for those who persecute you, so that you may be sons of your Father who is in heaven. For he makes his sun rise on the evil and on the good and sends rain on the just and on the unjust. For if you love those who love you, what reward do you have? Do not even the tax collectors do the same? And if you greet only your brothers, what more are you doing than others? Do not even the Gentiles do the same? You therefore must be perfect, as your heavenly Father is perfect. (Matthew 5:43-48 ESV)*

It is interesting that Christ had issue with the religious folks, but He never said that He hated them. He always sought a way to get revelation to them to change their paradigm, even the ones who persecuted Him. You cannot find any place where Jesus told them there was hatred in His heart toward them. Every single confrontation was done in love.

EVERY SINGLE CONFRONTATION WAS DONE IN LOVE

For us the biggest challenge is that we do not know how to deal with confrontation as it relates to our friends, our children, our parents or our spouses. Often, we fail to realize that confrontation can be OK. Not all confrontation is for destruction. When it reaches the point where there is anger and hatred toward someone – then it has become unhealthy and you have single handedly closed the door to prosperity in your social life. Remember prosperity is defined as the condition of being successful or thriving.

Let us look at an example of two people whose actions did not allow their "social life" to prosper. It is the story of two disciples who lost their focus on love amidst a disagreement.

Paul and Barnabas had a wonderful history of friendship. They traveled together, they both witnessed God moving in the midst of their ministries. In one of their trips, Barnabas' cousin accompanied them, and it was somewhat clear at the time, that missions were simply not his "cup of tea". We don't know the reason, we don't know the details, but in the middle of that trip John also known as Mark (Barnabas' cousin) decided to leave. In today's vernacular, he left Paul and Barnabas hanging out to dry, to complete the trip on their own. Time passed and they were preparing another missions trip, and what happened? Let us read for ourselves in Act 15:36-40:

> *Then after some days (*not from the previous trip just in context of Acts 15*) Paul said to Barnabas, "Let us now go back and visit our brethren in every city where we have preached the word of the Lord, and see how they are doing." Now Barnabas was determined to take with them John called Mark. But Paul insisted that they should not take with them the one who had departed from them in Pamphylia and had not gone with them to the work. Then the contention became so sharp that they parted from one another. And so Barnabas took Mark and sailed to Cyprus; but Paul chose Silas and departed, being commended by the brethren to the grace of God. (NKJV)*

They both had valid points, but neither were willing to reach a compromise to maintain and protect the friendship; in essence, their brotherhood. There is something that we must do to truly prosper in this area of our life. Ready? We must give up our right to be "right". For many this is the biggest challenge. Every conflict you have, has at its root, the desire to be affirmed in your points of disagreement. Nobody wants to take the responsibility of being incorrect.

In all the Bible following this event, we never see Paul and Barnabas speaking or traveling together again. They lost their focus on what had true value – their relationship.

So now you may ask, "OK, so how do I prosper in this area of my life?" Titus 3:1-7 says the following:

> *Remind them to be submissive to rulers and authorities, to be obedient, to be ready for every good work, to speak evil of no one, to avoid quarreling, to be gentle, and to show perfect courtesy toward all people. For we ourselves were once foolish, disobedient, led astray, slaves to various passions and pleasures, passing our days in malice and envy, hated by others and hating one another. But when the goodness and loving kindness of God our Savior appeared, he saved us, not because of works done by us in righteousness, but according to his own mercy, by the washing of regeneration and renewal of the Holy Spirit, whom he poured out on us richly through Jesus Christ our Savior, so that being justified by his grace we might become heirs according to the hope of eternal life. (ESV)*

This Word encourages us to comprehend the level of relationships we have and defend them. If the idiot devil can divide a knitting of the Lord – imagine the spiritual ramifications. In a divorce, if children are on the scene, the trauma to those children can (and usually will) affect them the rest of their lives. There is no real difference when division comes into our social relationships. Imagine what could have been? Imagine the miracles that could have occurred if Paul and Barnabas would have seen beyond their own pride and found a compromise to protect their relationship. You see, when we protect our relationships even amid conflict, we position ourselves to prosper. In doing this, I believe the favor of GOD will overshadow us like we have never seen before.

Later we find that the same Apostle Paul who had some disdain toward John Mark, refer to him as "profitable" to him in ministry. What happened in between these times? We do not know, however I believe Paul realized that he was knitted to John Mark and needed to defend the relationship EVEN in the shadow of John Mark's cousin, Barnabas.

2 Timothy 4:11 (KJV)

> *Only Luke is with me. Take Mark, and bring him with thee: for he is profitable to me for the ministry.*

In Colossians, the Apostle Paul tells the person he is writing to, if John Mark comes, receive him.

Colossians 4:10 (KJV)

> *Aristarchus my fellow prisoner saluteth you, and Marcus, sister's son to Barnabas, (touching whom ye received commandments: if he come unto you, receive him;)*

In Philemon 1:24 he refers to John Mark as a fellow laborer. This is what we must defend, relationships that will overcome conflict because they are a knitting of God to fulfill purpose and destiny.

OUR FINANCES

The fifth and last area of our lives where He desires to prosper us, is in finances. Yes, finances! God desires, as the Designer, that we be in a state of being successful or thriving, when it comes to our finances. Now, this is not solely in the act of receiving but also the stewardship of our finances. Again, to renew the mind concerning prosperity, this is only one-fifth of where God wants us to prosper in.

Ok so let's deal with the "pink elephant in the room". First, we must understand that money itself is not bad. To say that money is bad is the equivalent of saying that work is bad. Why? Every day you get up from your warm bed, get in your vehicle with or without coffee and travel to a place called "work". What for? To get paid at the end of the week for your labor. If you come from an immigrant family, more than likely one of the greatest motives for you to come into the United States is money. If the result of something is sin, then what you do to acquire it must also be sin or bad. Money is solely an instrument of exchange. God gets no glory in seeing one of His children and their family going through hunger because of a lack of funds.

The key item to deal with here is the LOVE of money. Let us look at the infamous scripture used to justify an erroneous mindset. The first one is 1 Timothy 6:10,17 (NKJV) which says:

> *For the love of money is a root of all kinds of evil, for which some have strayed from the faith in their greediness, and pierced themselves through with many sorrows. (v. 10)*
>
> *Command those who are rich in this present age not to be haughty, nor to trust in uncertain riches but in the living God, who gives us richly all things to enjoy. (v. 17)*

Many stay on verse 10 and never continue reading in context. In doing so they miss the continuation and culmination of the thought in verse 17. The Apostle Paul tells young Timothy, and us, to tell the rich of this world not to be arrogant nor put their confidence in riches but on God. Never was Timothy told – rebuke them for their money. Never was he exhorted to confront them because of their money. The issue was and is where the person placed their confidence.

Also noteworthy is that he does not say, tell the rich that they are sinners going to hell because they are rich. Now here is the clincher for anyone reading this, the scripture continues to say to put our confidence in God who provides for us richly (look at this) so that we can enjoy it. God supplies for us so that we can enjoy it, not put our confidence in it, but enjoy it.

The second scripture reference used erroneously is Hebrews 13:5 which says:

> *Let your conversation be without covetousness; and be content with such things as ye have: for he hath said, I will never leave thee, nor forsake thee. (KJV)*

It is worth noting that the well known scripture we use about God never leaving us or forsaking us is a prosperity scripture. Remember, prosperity is the condition of being successful or thriving. We must see that He says to avoid the LOVE of money, not that we refrain from getting it or that we stay without it. It is a declaration, if not warning, to free ourselves from the love of money followed by being happy with what we have. Then he concludes with a promise – He will never leave us or forsake us. To understand the depth of this scripture we must understand the context. Now when I speak of context, I am not speaking about 3-4 verses before and after the key verse, I am referring to the entire context of the entire letter written.

> **MONEY IS SOLELY AN INSTRUMENT OF EXCHANGE**

Many scholars believe it is the Apostle Paul who wrote the letter to the Hebrews. The Hebrew people were going through significant persecution for their faith. Before they converted, these were people of influence in society. The Hebrew people were at the point of abandoning their new-found faith, because they had not yet seen the manifestation of what they were hoping for. With all of this in mind, we now understand that the root issue was not even the love of money, but their confidence. This would be the very reason why the scripture ends with "He will never leave you or forsake you."

So, what is the love of money? What does that look like? The love of money is when a person, minimizes or places in lower priority the truly important items in their life, such as family, marriage and children at the altar of the dollar. Essentially the love of money is taking those important items and sacrificing them at the altar of greed for personal gain. The word "covetousness" used for "love" here is not fraternal love, nor is it unconditional love, it is the word translated to mean lust. Lust is a disorderly passion. It is also the propensity to the carnal delights, an unmoderated appetite for something. When there is an unmoderated appetite, or a propensity for carnal delight for money – there is then, a demonstration of the love of money.

Now in practical terms, this lust is manifested in some of the following examples:

- a married person who forgets about his/her family and works 3 jobs, not to supply the needs (needs required to run the household) but to get the material stuff in excess

- a person who leaves his devotional time to go to work a second or third job when there is no real need to

- a person who makes a decision SOLELY based on salary without regard to the impact on their calling or relationships

Yet in Christendom there has been something else on the flip side of this concept. It is the love of a false promise. I have heard it said, "If what you have does not supply your need then it is a seed." Every time I hear it now – I cringe. This phrase has become extremely dangerous and has caused many to sow financial seeds when they were not ordained to do so. I know I may be losing some readers here but please hear the heart behind this.

There is the tithe and the offering. Now where you specifically stand on those two is entirely up to you and beyond the scope of this book. I happen to believe strongly in the tithe. What I am referring to is the offering.

I believe that the Word shows me that my God, Yahweh, is a God of integrity. He has no problem that we call Him on His Word because He is not a man that He should lie. If He said it, He will do it. Since we are made in His likeness, the follow-up thought must then be, "If I said it then I must do it." I believe God wants us to operate in integrity, too. Here is what I mean in the context of this book: If I borrow $5,000 from a credit company to buy a sofa and TV, then enjoy sitting on that sofa while watching my Netflix programs –integrity tells me to pay first whom I owe. I believe God wants me to operate in integrity with my electric company and my mortgage lender because they trusted me and gave me their services/money. I benefit from them every time I use heat, air conditioning or come home to rest in my wonderful home. Here's the kicker, how can we expect God to bless the seed we sow, when what we are sowing is supposed to go to fulfill our word with the electric company? We, as ministers who believe in the tithe, tell people that the tithe is earmarked for God. I find it interesting, how we don't share that the other money is also earmarked for the electric company, gas company, car note, and mortgage payment that we have enjoyed. I believe it is this false mentality (of dysfunctional giving) and manipulation which has led to many having a hard heart about giving and saying pastors are just taking people's money.

Multiple times throughout scripture Jesus talks about failing the commandments – the issue here is all about integrity. When one operates in integrity the commandments are simple and can be fulfilled. Here are a few examples close to home. When I operate in integrity and fulfill my promise to my wife – there is no adultery. When I operate in integrity in my business finances, then there is no stealing. I want to call your attention to Matthew chapter 5. In this chapter, verses 23-26 Jesus says,

> *"So if you are presenting a sacrifice at the altar in the Temple and you suddenly remember that someone has something against you, leave your sacrifice there at the altar. Go and be reconciled to that person. Then come and offer your sacrifice to God. When you are on the way to court with your adversary, settle your differences quickly. Otherwise, your accuser may hand you over to the judge, who will hand you over to an officer, and you will be thrown into prison. And if that happens, you surely won't be free again until you have paid the last penny." (NLT)*

Let me explain. The context here is speaking of a debt (when someone has something against you) – this is why Jesus says you won't be free until you have paid the last penny. He said if you have a "debt" with your brother when you are about to leave an offering at the temple – go and fix that FIRST. Reconcile. In other words, fulfill what you said you would do.

We must dispel this erroneous mindset which says, "If what I have can't supply my need it's a seed," it is not scripture – it is not God's design.

God's design is to supply for every need and thereby placing us in a position to prosper in all areas of our lives. Christ spoke and did what the Father told Him to say and do. Of Jesus' parables, 39 in total, 11 of them speak directly toward money and finances. The theme of stewardship in the parable of the talents is one great example of this.

Deuteronomy 8:18 says the following:

> *You shall remember the Lord your God, for it is he who gives you power to get wealth, that he may confirm his covenant that he swore to your fathers, as it is this day. (ESV)*

What covenant is he speaking of? Hebrews 6:13-14 answers this:

> *For when God made a promise to Abraham, since he had no one greater by whom to swear, he swore by himself, saying, "Surely I will bless you and multiply you." (ESV)*

The word for blessing is not only "to extend a spiritual blessing" but it includes all that was paid for on the cross of Calvary. In 2 Corinthians 8:9, we are told Jesus was made poor so that we can become "rich" (prosperous).

In 1 Kings 3:7-15 we see the history of the heir of King David and what God Himself declared over him.

> *Now, O Lord my God, You have made Your servant king instead of my father David, but I am a little child; I do not know how to go out or come in. And Your servant is in the midst of Your people whom You have chosen, a great people, too numerous to be numbered or counted. Therefore give to Your servant an understanding heart to judge Your people, that I may discern between good and evil. For who is able to judge this great people of Yours?" The speech pleased the Lord, that Solomon had asked this thing. Then God said to him: "Because you have asked this thing, and have not asked long life for yourself, nor have asked riches for yourself, nor have asked the life of your enemies, but have asked for yourself understanding to discern justice, behold, I have done according to your words; see, I have given you a wise and understanding heart, so that there has not been anyone like you before you, nor shall any like you arise after you. And I have also given you what you have not asked: both riches and honor, so that there shall not be anyone like you among the kings all your days. So if you walk in My ways, to keep My statutes and My commandments, as your father David walked, then I will lengthen your days." Then Solomon awoke; and indeed it had been a dream. And he*

> *came to Jerusalem and stood before the ark of the covenant of the Lord, offered up burnt offerings, offered peace offerings, and made a feast for all his servants. (NKJV)*

God spoke to Solomon, son of David, in a dream and all that God said to him in that dream was fulfilled.

Apostle Paul in Philippians 4:18-19 says the following:

> *I have received full payment, and more. I am well supplied, having received from Epaphroditus the gifts you sent, a fragrant offering, a sacrifice acceptable and pleasing to God. And my God will supply every need of yours according to his riches in glory in Christ Jesus. (ESV)*

Paraphrasing, the Apostle Paul says, "God used you all to supply for me, and the same One who used you to bless me, will supply ALL that you need according to His riches in glory in Christ Jesus." Another reference to the full redemptive cost at the cross for us.

His "riches in glory" are simply the riches obtained by way of Christ's sacrifice on the cross. What are these riches in glory? That we be prosperous (in a condition of being successful or thriving) in these five areas of our life:

- Spirit
- Soul
- Body
- Social life
- Finances

It is time that the Body of Christ understand this and have a revelation concerning this being His will for us.

In the following chapters, we will discover more about the design of the One who supplies. Let's return to Eden to see how He supplies, in order to identify how we can prosper in our walk and these five areas of our life.

PROSPERITY DELUSION

III
The Genesis of Luxury

In summary we have learned the following so far: Prosperity is not money, nor is it measured in dollars and cents, it is the condition of being successful or thriving.

If Biblical prosperity is the condition of being successful or thriving, we must know where the starting point is. Essentially answering, where did this idea begin? The only way to identify growth or success is to understand where we start from. This is what I refer to as the genesis (beginning) of a thing.

In the book of Genesis chapter 2 verse 7-9 it depicts the following:

> And the Lord God formed man of the dust of the ground, and breathed into his nostrils the breath of life; and man became a living being. The Lord God planted a garden eastward in Eden, and there He put the man whom He had formed. And out of the ground the Lord God made every tree grow that is pleasant to the sight and good for food. The tree of life was also in the

> *midst of the garden, and the tree of the knowledge of good and evil. (NKJV)*

In verse 7 we learn that Adam was formed from the dust of the earth. In verse 8 the words "planted" or placed means to be established. God created a garden and then man was formed, and He PLACED or established Adam in said garden. Contrary to popular belief, Adam was created and THEN relocated into the garden. He was not created in Eden.

When Adam sinned, he was removed from the garden and returned to the place again from where he was first formed. In Genesis 3:23 we read it very clearly:

> *... therefore the Lord God sent him out of the garden of Eden to till the ground from which he was taken.*

This is important when we understand that in the garden is where everything was that he/they needed. In Genesis 2:15 he is given the mandate to work and keep the garden, which means utilize it for your benefit, then to keep it means to protect it, provide stewardship of what was entrusted.

Essentially God put Adam and Eve as keepers of the garden. Why? The garden had everything; the trees from which they could eat, and the one tree they could not eat from. It is interesting to note that although Adam was not created in the garden, Eve was. The ideal helpmate came from the place where God supplied everything for man.

Things were so good in the garden that God and Adam began to collaborate and name creation. Imagine, that! God, and His creation Adam, collaborating.

God designed Eden with a river that came from the garden and it divided into four branches, of which each one had its own riches.

Let us look at Genesis 2:9-14:

> *And out of the ground the Lord God made every tree grow that is pleasant to the sight and good for food. The tree of life was also amid the garden, and the tree of the knowledge of good and evil. Now a river went out of Eden to water the garden, and from there it parted and became four riverheads. The name of the first is Pishon; it is the one which skirts the whole land of Havilah, where there is gold. And the gold of that land is good. Bdellium and the onyx stone are there. The name of the second river is Gihon; it is the one which goes around the whole land of Cush. The name of the third river is Hiddekel; it is the one which goes toward the east of Assyria. The fourth river is the Euphrates. (NKJV)*

The first branch is called Pishon which signifies (look at this) increase! It sustained a place called Havilah where there was much gold. It is believed that the gold from this area was of exceptional quality. Also, in that same location were precious aromatics and onyx.

The second branch is called Gihon which means overflow. This river supplied for Cus which was considered a secular place. It is in this very place, where the story of Solomon we previously mentioned, occurred (the dream and promise from God).

The third river is the Tigris which means accelerated or fast and it sustained the land of Asyria.

The fourth is the Euphrates which means fruitful, productive. Euphrates is mentioned in Genesis 15:18 which is where God spoke to Abraham about the promise to him and his descendants.

> *On the same day the Lord made a covenant with Abram, saying: "To your descendants I have given this land, from the river of Egypt to the great river, the River Euphrates— (NKJV)*

It is mentioned again in Joshua 1:4-5, then again in Deuteronomy 11:24, when it says every place that your foot shall tread upon shall be yours. In 2 Samuel 8:3 David recovers his possessions from the coast of the Euphrates.

We had to analyze this because it is important to understand the genesis of luxury. If we understand the genesis of something, we can then understand the context of what happened before.

In Romans 5:12-19 the Apostle Paul is telling us something very important. He is giving us a summary of the timeline of Christ's sacrifice to the point of our restoration. You see many believe we are restored through Christ, but to what point in mankind's timeline? Where did Christ's resurrection restore us to? We all know He restored our relationship with God, however where can we find a description as to where He restored us? Well the answer is there in Romans 5:12-19, let's review:

> *Therefore, just as sin came into the world through one man, and death through sin, and so death spread to all men because all sinned for sin indeed was in the world before the law was given, but sin is not counted where there is no law. Yet death reigned from Adam to Moses, even over those whose sinning was not like the transgression of Adam, who was a type of the one who was to come.*
>
> *But the free gift is not like the trespass. For if many died through one man's trespass, much more have the grace of God and the free gift by the grace of that one man Jesus Christ abounded for many. And the free gift is not like the result of that one man's sin. For the judgment following one trespass brought condemnation, but the free gift following many trespasses brought justification. For if, because of one man's trespass, death reigned through that one man, much more will those who receive the abundance of grace and the free gift of righteousness reign in life through*

the one man Jesus Christ. Therefore, as one trespass led to condemnation for all men, so one act of righteousness leads to justification and life for all men. For as by the one man's disobedience the many were made sinners, so by the one man's obedience the many will be made righteous. (ESV)

Genesis 3 describes Adam's sin, where the law of sin and death was constituted. God had a plan from then to send someone that would redeem what was lost by Adam. Now through Jesus the Christ, we are made or declared righteous. Perhaps for some this may not seem to be a big deal. What I want us to get here is that through Jesus; by way of His sacrifice, the moment we accept Him as Savior, righteousness is restored. This means that there is no second judgment He has judged you righteous through the sacrifice of Christ. As it says in the letter to the Corinthians you are made a new creature. This means that you are made something new, you are "born-again". In other words, to make it very plain, through Christ God has hit the "reset button" on your life to start anew.

We are restored. The word restore is renewed, or to place something in its rightful state as it was before. We must comprehend that the only one who can restore us or place us BACK to the rightful state we were in before the fall of man is our Creator. He is the only one that knows the original plan and design we had before the foundations of the earth.

You may ask what this has to do with prosperity? What does restoration have to do with the condition of being successful or thriving? God so desires your prosperity that He has demonstrated it clearly in the act of sending Jesus; His only son.

Without redemption, we would remain in our sin. This would be a life without restoration or redemption. We would live a life trying to payback on our own for what Adam had done (like the law did).

Imagine life without the opportunity to be positioned again back to what the original Designer desired. Imagine asking forgiveness for an offense yet constantly feeling like you must earn it. I know many who live under the torment of how they messed up BIG in the past and yet feel they must pay some penitence still 20 years later.

Perhaps the question still remains as to what the original position is? Where is the original position that we are restored to? As human beings we are sent into the earth with what we call a sinful nature. This helps us understand the need for a redeemer. For some it takes 10 years on this earth for others 60. The beauty of it is that the redemption clause does not have an expiration date like a coupon (although as mentioned before, it's concept can be like a coupon). Our original designed position is that of being in relationship with the Father. This is the primary purpose of Jesus having come, to restore those who believe in Him and as a result, restoring relationship with the Father. To place us in a position of intimacy and codependency with the Father. To fully get an understanding we must return to the beginning.

The first Adam was created in friendship with God. He had intimacy, sharing, and co-laboring as some of the cornerstones of their relationship. To such a point, that they co-labored in naming creation. There was a partnership. One did not do anything without the other. There is something very interesting here – Adam came from the earth outside of Eden and was then placed in Eden. Now let's compare the first Adam, type and shadow of the last Adam (Jesus), who came from paradise or God's garden to earth. It had to happen this way to reciprocate what the first Adam did, in order for the last Adam to restore us back to paradise, the place called Eden where all is supplied.

When the disciples and Jesus had a conversation about prayer and how to do it, Jesus says to them that His Kingdom be fulfilled on earth as it is in heaven (not Jesus' kingdom, His Father's – which are one in the same but if He said his own that would have caused some issues).

Jesus was demonstrating to them the plan of restoration and the design of redemption. God's perfect plan to redeem us to the place of Eden, an allegory of the place where all needs are supplied. Yet not only that, but where you and I can walk and have conversations with our Creator just as easy as you are reading this very book. The place where we can co-labor with God so that His Kingdom will be done on earth as it is in heaven.

God the Father is your Designer. He has placed you on earth so that you prosper in Christ. Outside of Him there is a void which nobody or nothing can fill. He sent His Son so that we can have a life in abundance.

In John 10:9-10 the following words are shared for our edification and understanding:

> *I am the door. If anyone enters by Me, he will be saved, and will go in and out and find pasture. The thief does not come except to steal, and to kill, and to destroy. I have come that they may have life, and that they may have it more abundantly. (NKJV)*

Let us delve into the depth of this word to see that when we return to the beginning and have a clearer understanding, we can see God's design to prosper us in every area of our lives. In verse 9 the word "saved" means; to save, keep safe and sound, to rescue from danger or destruction; to deliver from the penalties of the Messianic judgment. The words "in" and "out" is a type and shadow of what Deuteronomy 28:6 says *"Blessed shall you be when you come in, and blessed shall you be when you go out."* Also, in John 10:9 "find pasture" is the Greek work "nome" which is: he shall not want the needful supplies for the true life; growth and increase. Sound familiar? Yes! It's prosperity, the condition of being successful or thriving.

We continue to verse 10 that says, the "thief" which according to the original text and contrary to popular belief, has nothing to do with the devil or enemy. It comes from the root of where we get kleptomaniac - an embezzler, pilferer; the name is transferred to false teachers, who do not care to instruct men, but abuse their confidence for their own gain. Now the rest of the words used are the following:

- Steal – to take the property of another wrongfully
- Kill – to sacrifice, immolate
- Destroy – render useless
- Life – a life active and vigorous, devoted to God, blessed
- Abundance – exceeding some number or measure or rank or need; over and above, more than is necessary, super-added, exceeding, abundantly, supremely; something further, more, much more than all, more plainly superior, extraordinary, surpassing, uncommon

What can we conclude from this? Let us translate (per the definitions and depth shared) and meditate on it. Let us use the original scripture and then add the definitions (essentially creating an amplified version).

> *I am the door. If anyone enters by Me (Christ), he will be saved (safe and sound, rescued from danger or destruction; delivered from the penalties of the Messianic judgment), and will go in and out (be blessed going in an out) and find pasture (shall not want the needful supplies for the true life; will grow and increase). The thief (embezzler, pilferer, NOT the devil) does not come except to steal (to take the property of another wrongfully), and to kill (sacrifice, immolate), and to destroy (render useless). I have come that they may have life (a life active and vigorous,*

devoted to God, be blessed), and that they may have it (life) more abundantly (exceeding some number or measure or rank or need; over and above, more than is necessary, superadded exceeding abundantly, supremely; something further, more, much more than all, more plainly superior, extraordinary, surpassing, uncommon).

Now in context Jesus is speaking about leadership, not the devil. He is saying that the leader who comes to steal, kill and destroy is a thief. He is not comparing Himself to the devil although the devil does steal, kill and destroy. Remember Jesus speaks about wolves and leaders, and says He is the door, or He is THE leader which guides us in the abundant life.

When you know your purpose, when you comprehend "why" you were born, then you will begin to prosper in all areas of your life. Christ came so that through Him as the leader in our life we can have an abundant life. Sadly, there are many in the church who give the power of their purpose and destiny to a leader to validate them, when the only validation they need is from Jesus.

> **THROUGH CHRIST, GOD HAS RESTORED YOU BACK TO THE PLACE OF EDEN**

Through Christ, God has restored you back to the place of Eden. In Eden all of Adam's needs were met and it is the same for us – an abundant life. Just like Adam, there will always be provision when we are attending to our assignment.

IV
The Quest for Provision

If I were to ask every person with a vision (a desired outcome), "What is the primary need that seems to be inhibiting your ability to make your vision a reality?" More than likely the answer would be (perhaps even 90% of the time), lack of provision such as money. Furthermore, a lack of provision in resources, not solely money but people, equipment and tools.

For every entrepreneur, pastor or corporate leader who desires to launch forth in anything – their biggest challenge is always provision. The inability for parents to send their children to college is often an issue of provision. For every man who simply wants to watch his favorite college team on a big screen TV, it is a question of provision. For every young person who wants to play sports, it is a question of required resources which again is – provision.

Each person has a vision, they have something that they desire to see come to fruition, something that may even rob them of sleep, and the only thing that is lacking most times is provision.

There was a man who did not have enough provision to take a dream vacation on a cruise ship. He began to save his "change" and even stopped from tithing to save for his cruise. When the time arrived, he went eagerly to the travel agency to purchase his ticket for the cruise. There was only one more month to the cruise date, but he finally accomplished it. He was on the brink of seeing his vision come to pass.

During that month, he thought, "I am going to save some canned goods to take with me on the cruise because I only have money for the cabin on the cruise."

> **THE ONLY THING THAT IS LACKING MOST TIMES IS PROVISION**

Finally, the day of the cruise arrived. Ecstatic, with all his clothes and his canned goods he arrived at the cruise ship. Every day for the 7-day cruise he happily ate in his cabin, choosing his meals from his inventory of canned goods. On the last day a cruise employee visited his cabin to find out if all was OK. He also wanted to make sure that the passenger did not miss the last day's party, which was available to all. When the man opened the door to welcome the cruise employee, he began to explain that he would not be going because he did not have the money to attend. The cruise employee, surprised at his explanation said, "Sir, surely you did not expect that the cruise line would charge you more for this event? In fact, all of the meals for the entire 7-day cruise were covered in the cost you paid with your ticket." Imagine the look on the passenger's face.

The ignorance of this man kept him from reaping the benefits prepared for him as a cruise passenger. He spent the entire time of his 7-day cruise in his room with canned goods because he perceived he would not have access to enjoy the lavish banquets. He was robbed of good food, making new friends and making new memories on his dream trip. Perhaps he did enjoy his limited experience. Maybe he did have a great time. Yet imagine how much more of a great time he would have had, if he had known all his benefits. The challenge is this – there are times in our own lives we are satisfied with something that appears to be just enough because we perceive God to be a "just enough God". However, He is more than just enough – He is an abundant God. He lavishes on His children!

In this chapter, let us look into three ways the Bible teaches us about provision. I do not claim to say these are all inclusive, rather they are simply three examples.

The first way is simply what I shared in the previous story – the provision is already there! Let's look at Joshua 18:1-6:

> *Now that the land was under Israelite control, the entire community of Israel gathered at Shiloh and set up the Tabernacle. But there remained seven tribes who had not yet been allotted their grants of land. Then Joshua asked them, "How long are you going to wait before taking possession of the remaining land the Lord, the God of your ancestors, has given to you? Select three men from each tribe, and I will send them out to explore the land and map it out. They will then return to me with a written report of their proposed divisions of their new homeland. Let them divide the land into seven sections, excluding Judah's territory in the south and Joseph's territory in the north. And when you record the seven divisions of the land and bring them to me, I will cast sacred lots in the presence of the Lord our God to assign land to each tribe. (NLT)*
>
> *This is the story of what happened after Joshua united the people and destroyed more than 50 nations to enter the*

> *promised land. The key here is – the "promised" land. This lets us know that someone had promised it already. It was already prepared for them and was awaiting them to take possession of it. I do not want to assume anything about my reader so to be clear, the person who promised it and prepared it was none other than God.*

After all of that conquering and dividing of the land there were still seven tribes that had not taken possession of the land that was theirs. We can only assume that perhaps it was because of laziness, fear, lack of interest or the big one that many hide behind – false humility. They may have thought they were not worthy. You see many of us, especially in the church, tend to think that denying ourselves of something is humility. However, when God provides you with something and you deny it because you think you are not worthy, it is more evidence of pride than anything else. It is also a slap to the face of God, who loves you and entrusts you with that provision. So, this then leads us to two items that are part of the provision:

1. The actual provision, the item promised

2. You taking ownership of it

We must comprehend just like the man on the cruise, that the God who has designed this provision thing, desires for us to take possession of what has been provided.

The second way is that the provision is already in you! Let's look at what 2 Kings 4:1-7 says:

> *One day the widow of a member of the group of prophets came to Elisha and cried out, "My husband who served you is dead, and you know how he feared the Lord. But now a creditor has come, threatening to take my two sons as slaves." "What can I do to help you?" Elisha asked. "Tell me, what do you have in the*

house?" "Nothing at all, except a flask of olive oil," she replied. And Elisha said, "Borrow as many empty jars as you can from your friends and neighbors. Then go into your house with your sons and shut the door behind you. Pour olive oil from your flask into the jars, setting each one aside when it is filled." So she did as she was told. Her sons kept bringing jars to her, and she filled one after another. Soon every container was full to the brim! "Bring me another jar," she said to one of her sons. "There aren't any more!" he told her. And then the olive oil stopped flowing. When she told the man of God what had happened, he said to her, "Now sell the olive oil and pay your debts, and you and your sons can live on what is left over." (NLT)

There are some key points we need to see there that are often overlooked. The husband of this woman was a prophet. With this we can estimate that her husband had prophesied over thousands of people in his life before dying. Yet we never hear of him prophesying over his family. This woman, mother and widow never knew that the possibility of the provision was in her. When someone called it out and declared the potential that was in her, a provision was manifested. She could then understand that her purpose was tied to her prosperity.

The story ends in a glorious manner. A kingdom business was created that not only paid her and her husband's debt, but also was sufficient for her and her family to continue living.

Many people underestimate the potential that is resident in them. Many minimize the talent that they have, yet it is very probable that the same talent can be a fountain of provision for their vision, and life.

The third way the Bible teaches us about provision is that the provision is generational. Let's look at Psalms 37:23-26.

> *The Lord directs the steps of the godly. He delights in every detail of their lives. Though they stumble, they will never fall, for the Lord holds them by the hand. Once I was young, and now I am old. Yet I have never seen the godly abandoned or their children begging for bread. The godly always give generous loans to others, and their children are a blessing. (NLT)*

The phrase "...begging for bread" is going through lack; being placed in a position where the lack is so great that the only alternative is begging. So, the writer of this Psalm is saying that in all his years he has never seen the godly and their children in that state. Now you may think, "Well today there is!" Or you may say, "I know some godly people and their children which are." The truth is you are right – there are. However, I must ask why? Is it because of lack of stewardship? Is it because of not knowing that God has provided? Is it not tapping into what He has given them as a talent and they think that they cannot use it to prosper? Here, the key item in this scripture is "godly". For most of us we look at that word and think a holy person, a sanctified person. The actual definition in context is a person who is right and just in his cause. So, it leads to the intention of the heart. What he is saying is that he has not seen a man who has the right intentions in his heart go through lack nor his children begging for bread.

We must continue to remind ourselves that the promises of God are indeed our provision. God has given us promises. I have learned early in my walk to make scripture personal, and one of the scriptures I do that with is Deuteronomy 28. When I do it reads like this (a portion only):

> *Because I fully obey the Lord my God and carefully keep all his commands that He gives me today, the Lord my God will set me high above all the nations of the world. I will experience all these blessings because I obey the Lord my God:*

My towns and my fields will be blessed.

My children and my crops will be blessed...

Now in that same book and chapter verses 11-14 let's read what it says:

> *The Lord will give you prosperity in the land he swore to your ancestors to give you, blessing you with many children, numerous livestock, and abundant crops. The Lord will send rain at the proper time from his rich treasury in the heavens and will bless all the work you do. You will lend to many nations, but you will never need to borrow from them. If you listen to these commands of the Lord your God that I am giving you today, and if you carefully obey them, the Lord will make you the head and not the tail, and you will always be on top and never at the bottom. You must not turn away from any of the commands I am giving you today, nor follow after other gods and worship them. (NLT)*

So now you may wonder, "Now what? You gave me all of this information and have had me captivated until now, but how do I put these principles in practice?" How do we practice and live out true prosperity (the condition of being successful or thriving)?

When we were children, we had something that could transport us around the world in moments. This "thing" we had was limitless. Although others around us may have also had it; the way we utilized it was always different than the way others used it. When we were children or even as youths, we could visualize something that would transport us into that vision to not only see it, but feel it. Perhaps you do not recognize what I am referring to. It is the place where we develop our dreams.

What about when we were children and our little matchbox car that measured 2" x 5" became not only a hot rod but an invincible car? It could jump 100's of feet (in its own scale comparison) and keep driving like nothing. It could flip multiple times, land on its wheels every time and continue driving like nothing happened. This was a result of our imagination.

If you are a woman, in your adolescence you may have pictured yourself in your wedding dress and about to marry the love of your life. You would take his hand and dance without a care in the world. Perhaps you would see your mother cooking in the kitchen and imagine yourself cooking for your own family one day.

So, the question is, "NOW WHAT?" Start to dream again. Dream in big ways. The only difference here is that now you have a real ally to make that dream a reality. First and foremost – Jesus. He is the one that is depositing that dream in you. He is the one who is pushing you to believe big. And even to ASK BIG. Scripture gives us great examples that we often overlook. For example, Joshua asked God to stop the sun from setting so that they could win the battle. Many just pass that by as a simple event. However, remember the sun does not move! The reality of the request is this: He was asking God to stop the rotation of the planetary system. Of which God did not say, "You are asking too big! You faith people are too much!" NO – He said, "Yes, I can do that, and I will do it."

If you have not done it – take the first step.

If you are ready to believe it, tell the Father in your own words – I am ready to believe BIG. Give me direction and a vision that takes me out of my comfort zone and pushes me to see that greater is He that is in ME than he that is in the world.

Submit to Him in all areas of your life and let Him give form to the dream in you by way of His word and Spirit. He never promises anything that would be easy to accomplish, because then you would not need Him. Yet He does promise that if we live by what He has said, we will be able to see the fruits in our life manifest and be provided for, prosperous and blessed.

If you have taken the first step, then the question continues to be – "Now what?" I would love to answer that using the words of Jesus in John chapter 6 verses 28-29:

> They replied, "We want to perform God's works, too. What should we do?" Jesus told them, "This is the only work God wants from you: Believe in the one he has sent." (NLT).

The ONLY work God expects from you is to solely BELIEVE. Believe in the One He has sent. Believe that He is for you not against you. Believe that the process is not for your destruction but for your growth and success.

The prosperous life is a life where you can believe that there is provision for everything you need. If you need wisdom, so that your soul prospers, and you make right decisions – the provision is there (James 1:5; 3:17). If you need information on how to change your eating habits so that your physical body can prosper – provision is there (1 Cor. 6:19-20). If you think you are an introvert and lack knowing how to communicate with people – the provision is already there (Ex. 4:10-12, Phil. 4:6-7). If you need a way to stretch your finances or a business idea so that your finances be prosperous – the provision is there (Deut 8:18, Hab. 2:2, Luke 14:28).

> **I AM READY TO BELIEVE BIG**

I do not pretend to give you a clear answer to every situation, but I do know where to point you to.

We must reach the point where we decide, that what the Word of God says is the final authority in our lives. Circumstances, arguments, doubt and insecurity, are not the final word. As a believer in this walk, the One who has the ultimate and final Word is the King of Kings, the Lord of Lords, the Beginning and the End, the Great I AM.

Provision according to its definition is something provided; a measure taken beforehand to deal with a need. For example, we know that God has called every single person. He has called each of us to a purpose, a design, and a function. This call was placed on us BEFORE the foundations of the world (see the book of Jeremiah). When God made the call or purpose on our lives, He already made provision for that to be fulfilled. I believe this is the reason you were born exactly when you were born – versus being born back in 1866. Provision is NOT SOLELY MONEY; it is the equipping, and enablement infused into you to fulfill His purpose on this earth. Often in Christian language we say, "that person is anointed". What we are truly saying is that he or she has discovered that there is provision given from God for him or her to fulfill their design or purpose!

Provision is the sustaining agent and resource for the vision. It truly is the "HOW" you can prosper – to be successful or thriving and accomplish your vision. In addition to the "how" is the "where". We must understand also, that provision is not only connected to a person, it is connected to a place.

V
There Is A Place

The place or location where God chooses to manifest Himself is a wonder to all believers. The questions like, why this town? Why this family? Why this church? God is centrally focused on locations. He is not interested in real estate, as much as He is the location to where He leads His people. In fact in the church today, there are names of God that reveal His character. Many have placed names on God that never originated from Him but rather from an event or location.

Traditionally there exists seven revelatory names of God. Here are some:

Exodus 3:14 - Yahweh - the existing One (more specifically: I AM WHO I AM)

Exodus 15:26 - Yahweh Rapha - the Lord who heals

Jeremiah 23:6 - Yahweh Tsidkenu - the Lord our righteousness

In contrast, these examples are names of locations:

Judges 6:24 - Yahweh Shalom - the Lord is Peace

Exodus 17:15 - Yahweh Nissi - the Lord is my banner

Ezekiel 48:35 - Yahweh Shammah - the Lord is there

Places or locations have always been important to God. Some examples of important places or locations for God are Gethsemane, the tabernacle, the road to Damascus and the pool of Bethesda.

Since these locations are important to God, they should also be important to the Body of Christ. For example, your church's location is a special place where you gather to hear the word of God for your life. Your place of prayer is another important location, because it is also where you are able to hear the voice of your Father.

There is a location that is often referred to as a 7th name of God, that in fact is not a name but a place. It is the famous Jehovah Jireh. The history of this name is very important, in order to understand the place and the value this has in our discussion about prosperity.

Genesis 17:19 speaks of a covenant or pact that God made with Abraham:

> *God said, "No, but Sarah your wife shall bear you a son, and you shall call his name Isaac. I will establish my covenant with him as an everlasting covenant for his offspring after him. (ESV)*

From what we can see and read; Isaac was born in a place called Canaan. Later for the Israelites, this location came to be known as their promised land, per the promise and prophecy that God gave Abraham in Genesis 17:8. This was part of the same conversation between God and Abraham concerning the arrival of his son Isaac.

Now in all the history of Abraham and his walk to the place of sacrifice, we never see Abraham speaking of death. We see in Genesis 22:5-6 the following:

> *Then Abraham said to his young men, "Stay here with the donkey; I and the boy will go over there and worship and come again to you." And Abraham took the wood of the burnt offering and laid it on Isaac his son. And he took in his hand the fire and the knife. So they went both of them together. (ESV)*

Now, was Abraham lying when he told them that they would come again to them? After all, he knew what God had asked him to do. Nonetheless, this did not hinder him from believing that the harvest that he received in his son was now a sacrificial seed. Many think this is a type and shadow of Jesus and God the Father, of which I can agree but I also believe that the explanation is much deeper. What if God wanted to know if the harvest He had given Abraham had become his god? What if God wanted to know if Isaac had become greater than the One who promised him.

All of this, yet Abraham had the confidence and conviction that God was going to provide another sacrifice. Again, knowing that his harvest manifestation in Isaac was called to be a seed.

On the walk, after Abraham's conversation with his people, Isaac turns to his dad and asks, "Dad, we got the wood, we got what we need but what about the sacrifice?" Imagine having to field that question, knowing that the one asking the question is indeed the sacrifice! Abraham made a proclamation of faith, "God will provide the sacrifice." Now the original of that text does not refer to the future, it was translated that way. It is past tense, in other words a true translation would read as – God has provided a sacrifice.

According to what the scripture says, they went to a mountain far away. This mountain is called Mount Moriah. Even though the

Bible says to go to the mountains of Moriah, the original text does not make use of the plurality of the word mountains but singular. This is a significant location because this is where Solomon will later build the temple he is known for. Moriah means "chosen of God".

> **ABRAHAM NAMES THE PLACE YAHWEH-YIREH**

So, there they were, both of them ready for the sacrifice. Abraham prepared the altar, and his son Isaac on it. We can only imagine how each of them were feeling; the thoughts running through their minds; the tears rolling down their faces. Abraham raised the knife to sacrifice his son at the place that God has chosen (Moriah) and at that moment an angel appeared and says to Abraham, "STOP do not kill the child!" In the following instant Abraham lifted his head and there, stuck in the thicket, was the sacrifice that would replace Isaac. It was a ram not a sheep, this is important because the sacrificial ram is different than the sheep. Jewish tradition makes the distinction between the two as simply a sheep being a young animal and a ram a mature animal. This is a type and shadow of Jesus, who was not sacrificed as a child but a mature man.

It is in Genesis 22:14 where we see that Abraham named the location (NOT God):

> *And Abraham called the name of that place Jehovahjireh: as it is said to this day, In the mount of the Lord it shall be seen. (KJV)*

> *Abraham named the place Yahweh-Yireh (which means "the Lord will provide"). To this day, people still use that name as a proverb: "On the mountain of the Lord it will be provided." (NLT)*

Did you catch it? Abraham names the PLACE, Yahweh-Yireh (Jehovahjireh). Again, it is not that he named the Creator such, moreover that he called the PLACE Yahweh-Yireh because the Lord provided. Remember the mountain named Moriah means "chosen of God".

In summary we can capture the following:

1. In the place that God has chosen, He supplied a sacrifice for His friend, Abraham.

2. In turn Abraham called the PLACE where God supplied Yahweh-Yireh.

3. We now must understand that it is not a name of God, rather a location. It is the place where decisions of faith are made, where you will be prospered in every area of your life.

There are so many who desire to prosper (experience the condition of being successful or thriving) but they never take the time to ask, "Lord is this my Jehovahjireh, is this the place where You will provide?" Is this my Moriah? Perhaps this does not sound to practical to you for today.

For practical purposes, let's put this in today's terms. "Lord is this job my Jehovahjireh?" Or, "Lord is this church my Moriah?" If only these questions would be posed and we would await the answer, we might be able to avoid many of the pitfalls that occur in our lives. This could truly put us in a place where we can experience the condition of being successful or thriving.

The church decision is probably one of the largest one's we miss the mark on in this day and age. We think we have the right to choose what church to go to. Abraham did not choose which mountain to go to. What if he decided to go to another location that God had not chosen? What if he said to himself, that place is too far I'll just go over here down the road because I can't walk that far? I have said the following statement many times and will continue to share it the same way I heard the Lord tell me – ready?

There is no scripture in the entire Bible that gives us the right to choose where we go to church NOR who is to be our pastor. He places us. In the same way we do not get to choose the home we grow up in or the parents we are given.

Many of us would be living in a much better place if we understood this concept. Now keep in mind, I am not saying that seasons do not end however the departure should not be based on, "I wonder what that church is like?" It should and MUST be, "Lord, where is my Moriah? Where is the place you want me to establish myself anew?"

In scripture there are other places that can be "classified" as a Jehovahjireh.

In Matthew chapter 9 verses 20-21, we see the example of the woman with the issue of blood.

> *And suddenly, a woman who had a flow of blood for twelve years came from behind and touched the hem of His garment. For she said to herself, "If only I may touch His garment, I shall be made well." (NKJV)*

I have seen and even directed plays (as a youth pastor) that paint this very scene. At that moment she touched the hem of the garment of Jesus she was healed. Listen closely, at this moment was NOT when she was healed. This is solely when we see or hear of the manifestation of her healing. The moment she realized that there was a visitation going to occur at that location, she believed she would take part of that visitation and she would be healed. She "reserved" her healing the moment she heard and recognized that this could and would be a Jehovahjireh for her. It would be a place of supply and prosperity (the condition of being successful or thriving). Believing for your miracle is the preamble to the manifestation of that miracle. There is no faith exercised when the miracle is already manifested. The faith "muscle" is used when we believe for the miracle amidst the challenges.

Another example of Jehovahjireh or a location where God supplies is found in Mark 10:46-50:

> Now they came to Jericho. As He went out of Jericho with His disciples and a great multitude, blind Bartimaeus, the son of Timaeus, sat by the road begging. And when he heard that it was Jesus of Nazareth, he began to cry out and say, "Jesus, Son of David, have mercy on me!" Then many warned him to be quiet; but he cried out all the more, "Son of David, have mercy on me!" So Jesus stood still and commanded him to be called. Then they called the blind man, saying to him, "Be of good cheer. Rise, He is calling you." And throwing aside his garment, he rose and came to Jesus. (NKJV)

Bartimaeus was classified as blind. At this time every person who was sickly or gravely ill would wear a mantle that let everyone know that the person was sick in some way or form. When Jesus called him, the FIRST thing he did was to let go of the mantle that identified him as ill. He let go of his limitations, his mantle of condemnation, his mantle of rejection – God through His son Jesus had supplied a need at that place – a roadside on the way out of Jericho. In New Testament times Jericho stood some distance to the south-east of the ancient one, and near the opening of the valley of Achor. It was a rich and flourishing town, having a considerable trade, and celebrated for the palm trees which adorned the plain around.

> **BELIEVING FOR YOUR MIRACLE IS THE PREAMBLE TO THE MANIFESTATION OF THAT MIRACLE**

As we can see, there are many other examples, such as the pool at Bethesda (John 5). Nothing happened for that man until

God showed up by way of Jesus. That was his Jehovahjireh.

Your Jehovahjireh can very well be the place you are currently reading this. Your soul is being prospered and supplied of many answers to questions you may have had for so long.

Just like Abraham, perhaps you thought that you were obedient in doing something, but God has brought this book into your hands in this very place to provide you with something. Something that impacts your life forever.

Right where you are, in this moment ask the Lord, "Lord is this my Jehovahjireh? Is this the place where You are calling me, where my needs will be met and I and will prosper in every area of my life? Lord allow me to perceive what you are doing and see things the way you see them not how I perceive them…"

VI
Perception - What Do You See?

Every single one of us searches to know, "What is going to happen tomorrow?" People spend money going to psychics and astrologists to be able to capture a glimpse of tomorrow.

We are obsessed with the possibility of knowing what the future holds for us, and what we need to do to get there. Many times, we do not receive all God has for us, and the fact is that it is not God's fault nor the devil's. The reality is that many of us self-destruct. We become obscured from the possibilities due to our own decisions, fears, and insecurities.

In Numbers 13 of the Bible, there is something very interesting concerning this thought pattern. Many of us would be in the very same place we are now – regardless of whether "the devil did it" or not. We do a great job of messing things up ourselves. The reason being, we refuse to embrace what God desires for us because it seems impossible, and the reality is – it is impossible.

In Numbers 13:32-33 here is what we read:

> *So they spread this bad report about the land among the Israelites: "The land we traveled through and explored will devour anyone who goes to live there. All the people we saw were huge. We even saw giants there, the descendants of Anak. Next to them we felt like grasshoppers, and that's what they thought, too!" (NLT)*

One of the most powerful principles that we can discover, is the ability to see things through the perception of how God sees them. Perception is powerful. Perception can open doors of favor quickly or close them just as quick. Perception can cause a miscommunication between two persons or build a strong knitting among people that can last for years. I always share that your perception is your current reality. The way you perceive things, friends, circumstances or finances is your reality. Your current reality is entirely based on how you perceive every single area of your life.

You are alone, because you perceive that there is nobody out there. You are broke, because you perceive that the money you are getting is not enough even before you receive it. Your marriage is in trouble because you perceive that there is no way it can be fixed. Your reality right now is based on the results of your past perceptions in that area of your life.

In life we are received by people through the way we are perceived. Certain circumstances may have nothing to do with racism, but everything to do with how we allow people to perceive us. Yet here is the reality about perception – it does not have to be true. In fact, most times it may not be true or fact based. It is usually based on a statistical reality that a person has of people who dress, look, talk, move and present themselves like you.

Biblically this is made clear when we look at Jesus and His

encounter with the Samaritan woman near the well of Jacob. Jesus is the personification of the five-fold ministry. He is an Apostol, Prophet, Evangelist, Pastor and Teacher all wrapped into one. He was these then and He is these now. In John chapter 4, He found Himself with a woman who "happened" to be Samaritan and started a conversation with her about her life. He told her to go and get her husband. Her reply, "I don't have a husband." In today's vernacular it would have sounded like, "I ain't got a man." Jesus responded, "You're right you don't have a husband, but you have five guys and none of them are your husband." Then she makes a statement that is so interesting because to many of us today, it would have been obvious. She said, "I perceive that you are a prophet." Again, remember she is a Samaritan. No religious upbringing, no clear conviction of the Torah, yet she perceives Jesus to be a prophet. Often, we read that and think from the mindset of a Christian but she was not. In fact, the Samaritan and the Jew were at odds with each other culturally.

Here is a woman whose life was radically changed because her perception had changed. She ran and told others of her experience and she left sinning no more, as per Jesus' instruction.

In the case of Nicodemus, he approached Jesus and told Him that he KNEW that Jesus came to teach and show them something (John 3). He perceived that Jesus had come for this mission and call.

Here is the challenge my dear brother/sister - you can read this book and many others after it on any subject to help you in your walk. This is a great idea and is needed, I would never tell you different. However, until you decide to change the perception of a thing, then the way you BELIEVE about that same thing will never change. Your perception precedes your belief.

You had to get to a point of perceiving the need of a Savior before you believed you needed one. In our walk, we then must work out the perception that this overall obedience thing is a tight rope act and that if we slip off the rope God will strike us down. (Parenthetically speaking, let me tell you – your slipping is not that powerful.) When our perception or how we perceive this changes, then the way we believe about it will change resulting in a faith that can move mountains.

The problem with religion is that we think that if we can change the way someone acts, then they can come to the Lord. Yet behavior modification never results in the image of Christ being manifested in someone's life. The result of this behavior modification process or requirement is a religious mindset. It creates a life based on a forced set of rules and regulations that have people walking on a tight rope and never experiencing the grace of God.

> **PERCEPTION MAY LIMIT US FROM SEEING THE HAND OF GOD MOVE ON OUR BEHALF**

There are so many leaders in today's Church that try to force the modification of people's behaviors with these rules and the result is a congregation of slaves and orphans – not sons and daughters who understand the love and grace of the Father in their lives. The primary challenge with this is that they never realize they are a child of the King. You can take the child of a king and place that child in an environment where they are enslaved. They could live their life under the perceived identity of a slave. The child will comport themselves as a slave, react as a slave, and if not changed, raise their children as slaves. They know nothing different even though that child was the child of a king. Biblical perspective needed? Well look at Moses and Mephibosheth. Until their perception was corrected, they were each living as something other than their true identity. Although Moses was raised in the "lap of luxury" he spent many years as a fugitive in the wilderness. Years passed before being called to lead Israel out of Egypt. When his perception of God changed, Moses became the liberator of an entire nation. Mephibosheth was an actual grandchild of a king. He perceived that all was lost and that the reigning king, David, was going to kill him. Being dropped as a child left him lame and crippled his thinking. He saw himself as a dead dog and who needs that? However, Mephibosheth's perception changed after King David returned to him all that belonged to his grandfather and family. He was also given a place at the king's table.

The fact is that our current perception may limit us from seeing the hand of God move on our behalf in every circumstance, until it undergoes a change. And bless God I believe it is starting to happen right now as you read this!

Remember Nicodemus, we mentioned him earlier? Jesus tells him that nobody could enter the Kingdom of God without being born-again and by the Spirit.

Jesus was not telling him, "If you never confess the sinner's prayer, you will not see heaven or Saint Peter." Jesus was telling him that until you have a personal encounter with the Spirit of God, you will never understand what is happening in your life and what God is trying to get into your hands.

If you are not born-again, you will never be able to understand or perceive the Kingdom of God. You will think and believe that your challenges are "just circumstances," and never notice that it can be a divine strategy.

The biggest challenge in you today is who you think you are based on another's opinion or who you were before. Those other false identities are the biggest challenge to understanding who you are now. Think about how God sees you based on Bible truth versus how you perceive He sees you.

Look, if you have been in the Lord for some time you know that the devil can try to tempt you with things from the past, however they may not be as tempting as before. The desire to do certain things has ended. The attraction to that lifestyle may have left.

Again, the biggest challenge is knowing who you are NOW based on how God sees you. Let me share a secret – any and all temptations that may come from the devil will always challenge who you are or who you are about to become.

Let me explain. Finances are tight. You begin to try to move things around and juggle. The temptation comes to steal money. The issue is not the stealing, it is who you will become if you start to truly believe that He cannot and will not supply your need. The issue is you coming to the realization that worry is no longer your portion but a new found confidence in God has now shown you that you are not a failure, you are not stressed, you are blessed and highly favored.

We must understand that GOD did not create us for an experience. He did not create you or me to simply have a goose bump experience. Let me say this, at church there is much more than four songs, an offering, a sermon and departure prayer. God did not create you or the ministry you either lead or are a part of to lock Himself in to one experience. He created it all so that you can fulfill your purpose and the purpose of that ministry. You may think, "I'm not a pastor, so what is this about ministry?" Colossians 3 from the New Living Translation puts it clearly in verse 23, *"Work willingly at whatever you do, as though you were working for the Lord rather than for people."* You must comprehend that whatever we do as unto the Lord is ministry. Ministry by definition, is service and nothing more. As you do things for others as unto the Lord, you are doing it "as though you were working for the Lord." This is ministry. You are allowing yourself to be used by the Father (as unto the Lord) to bless someone else and their ministry (their public service).

When were you created? Before the foundations of the earth. When did He make a plan for you? Before the foundations of the earth. What is the first step of discovering that plan?

In other words, He created you; He created your church, your business, your profession, to fulfill and put a "period" to the reason Jesus was sent to the earth.

God says in Isaiah 55:8-13:

> "My thoughts are nothing like your thoughts," says the LORD. "And my ways are far beyond anything you could imagine. For just as the heavens are higher than the earth, so my ways are higher than your ways and my thoughts higher than your thoughts. "The rain and snow come down from the heavens and stay on the ground to water the earth. They cause the grain to grow, producing seed for the farmer and bread for the hungry. It is the same with my word. I send it out, and it always produces fruit. It will accomplish all I want it to, and it will prosper everywhere I send it. You will live in joy and peace. The mountains and hills will burst into song, and the trees of the field will clap their hands! Where once there were thorns, cypress trees will grow. Where nettles grew, myrtles will sprout up. These events will bring great honor to the LORD's name; they will be an everlasting sign of his power and love." (NLT)

One of my favorite scriptures! It summarizes all we have shared together in this book. First He says the way you think is not the way He thinks. And the way He does things is far beyond what you can imagine or perceive. Then He gives us a clear comparison that passes the test of time and culture. The goal is to get us to change the way we perceive Him. The punchline – God says it is the same with His Word. He sends it out and it ALWAYS produces fruit. It will accomplish all He wants it to, and it will prosper; be successful or thriving everywhere He sends it.

You see, you and I are that Word. Jesus was the Word as per John, we are co-heirs with Jesus and so we are His Word. God spoke a Word about you – and that WORD is greater than what we can perceive yet, it has been sent out to fulfill and prosper everywhere it is sent.

So now the question I would ask is, do you desire to do all that God has for you?

I have learned that God is obligated to cause things in your life to lead you to a place where you come to the end of you. To get to the point where you say, "Lord I cannot any longer, this is too much." The goal is not to destroy us physically, but to really allow us to depend on Him. We are in what psychologists call, a "co-dependent" relationship with God.

This codependency is based on a mutual benefit and submission. This is why submission is such a key word in scripture. It is the willingness to let go of your own preference for someone else's. Some would call this a sacrifice; however, a sacrifice is a substitution for something else, it is a tool used for redemption. Codependency has no sacrifice involved because it is based on a mutual dependency.

This willingness to submit allows us to further understand scriptures that say, "let the weak say I am strong." It is through this submission of our will to His, that we are made strong. It is in our weakness He is made strong. We reach the point of saying as one famous singer said, "Jesus take the wheel."

It is in this place where His favor shines through. Where His grace is at an absolute abundance, setting us up to be successful and thriving.

It is sad that we have relegated prosperity to be a hot concept. A new evangelical move spearheaded by a few great ministers.

Prosperity in its truest definition requires PROCESS. The only way we can be successful or thrive is through changing. Changing old paradigms, and rethinking things through new eyes. This delusion of prosperity has caused us to go to an extreme. The result is that we have become great – even AMAZING – dreamers, but horrible implementors of the principles that can take us to the place of seeing the manifestation of that great dream.

We must become aware and keen to the fact that the process cannot be avoided, and it will not be something we can skip. The principle of God's prosperity is not a get rich quick scheme. It is not multi-level marketing, and surely is not solely dollars and cents. It is not measured in what material things we can accumulate, and it is not governed by the social political climate of our day. It is governed by the excellent Designer of the principles. It is measured in the very place where the Designer resides – the heart of man. Many of us have this notion of thinking that God is going to run to us when we are uncomfortable. The fact is that He never promised comfort – He provides a process and delineates it in His will. When we are a new babe in Christ perhaps that is the case. However as we grow in our walk, He rightfully expects us to learn and learn by the process intertwined into the design. The goal is that we reflect our big brother – Jesus.

> **PROSPERITY IN ITS TRUEST DEFINITION REQUIRES PROCESS**

Your future has always been in your present. What you are willing to let go of today will reveal what God can put in your hands tomorrow. You are today the results of the decisions you made yesterday and will be tomorrow the results of the decisions you make today.

So, you are now in a place of decision. You are now faced with a decision to make that has the potential to forge your future into one that is successful and thriving. Yet the choice is always yours. This is that codependency thing. He won't force you. He will give you opportunity after opportunity, but He will never force you. Yet here is a key, if you find yourself over and over "hitting the gas" but going nowhere – could it be that the problem is not God or the devil but you?

The fact is that when God decides to promote or take someone to a place of prosperity (the condition of being successful or thriving) in all five areas of life – He is not obligated to announce it to you three days before. He is not obligated to notify you one hour before. The fact is that He will do it in HIS timing.

If you take anything from this book, take this – You are no longer a miserable failure worth nothing. You are no longer that child in the corner crying wondering, "Why?" You are no longer that man who stays up at night trying to figure out solutions to problems. You are no longer that woman who fears starting a business because of past failures. You are, as per God's words which He released (in accordance with Isaiah 55), a son or daughter of the King. You are a priest called with a holy calling to impact a home, community, state, region, nations and a world with the truth that the design of God who supplies is prosperity Himself!

Finally, what is the delusion for you?

One of the definitions Webster's has for delusion is to mislead the mind or judgment of; a false belief or opinion. In Psychiatry, delusion is a fixed false belief that is resistant to reason or confrontation with actual fact. The popular belief of what prosperity is has become steeped in a tradition of thinking that God only is giving cash handouts to people. For some reason we have reached the point of thinking that God is in heaven and we have become His welfare project, His needy children who constantly need money for gas and food. His design for prosperity is for us to enter a place of success and thriving in our lives entirely – not just money or material goods. In that design of prosperity does He desire to give us "things"? Yes, but not just things. He gives us what we need to walk out this gift and call in our lives, truly causing His word (us) to prosper. In doing so, we can put finality to a myth that says Christians are always _____ (you fill it in now that you know what the myth is and what prosperity truly is).

Here is my prayer for you:

Father, I lift my brother / sister, as Your son /daughter before You. I declare and decree this book to be an instrument to spark a deeper journey in Your Word. A deeper desire to truly seek prosperity as You have designed it - not how we have defined it.

Lord, we submit ourselves to Your will, Your desire, Your plan, Your calling, Your gifting in us as we go about this journey. We thank You for wisdom, as You have said through Your servant – if anyone lacks wisdom let him ask and YOU will give it without reproach. Lord we understand this wisdom may be challenging to our mindsets, but Your thoughts are higher than ours. We declare that amidst the challenges and Your higher thoughts for us, that favor is set before us in our walk. I believe our gift will put us before great men as we prosper in every area of our life, spirit, soul, body, finances and socially with one another in the faith. Amen.

About the Author

Dr. Marc Garcia has been in relationship with the Lord since the age of 22 (Since May,1994) after serving 4 years in the US Navy.

He has served in ministry departments from preteen ministry director, youth ministry director, chaplain, men's ministry director. He has an earned Doctorate in Biblical Studies from North Carolina College of Theology.

For more than 13 years Dr. Marc has produced, directed and edited a TV program called Home Team (now called Dominion Today) where he and his wife speak on topics such as marriage, family, and leadership.

He and his wife Blanca (of 20 years - since 2000) have a 25 year old son and demonstrate the Father's heart in becoming Foster parents. They live in Lyman, SC and attend a local church in Spartanburg.

They have church planted and now lead The Bridge Ministries, a para-church ministry that assists pastors and ministry leaders in organization and structure. Dr. Marc also leads the first bilingual family friendly TV station in the country called Vida Family. (www.vida-tv.com) as well as a content marketing company called NVMedia (www.nuevavida.media)

If you would like to contact Dr. Marc Garcia please feel free to email him @ drmgarcia@bethebridgesc.org or his various social media pages: (IG: @DrMarcGarcia; TW: @DrMarcGarcia; LinkedIn: /in/drmarcgarcia)

PERSONAL NOTES:

Left blank intentionally

Left blank intentionally

www.ingramcontent.com/pod-product-compliance
Lightning Source LLC
Chambersburg PA
CBHW071315060426
42444CB00036B/3032